Let's Help Each Other

* Can You Relate to These Stories*

About the Author:

Lakyshia L (Shelton) Hubert (25) was born in Pahokee Florida and raised In Clewiston Florida! She is the youngest of her six siblings (and a host of step brothers and sisters that her parents helped raise over the years)! In 2013 Lakyshia and her mother Mary (Shelton) joined together and published two Poetry books called Poetry of Life Part one and two. Lakyshia is also a loving wife and mother of two young sons.) While reading this book it's going to get very emotional yet very interesting. The lust of young love, what older folks would call puppy or blind love leading to a lifetime of pain! The pleasure of intercourse can lead to a lifetime of pain. Some of the things you'll read are about the author, some are about different people, the diseases, the story, and the life of the streets, etc... I'm bringing these stories out because I want to reach out to you young girls, boys, women, and men. Whomever these stories may be able to help! Sometimes you feel as if you're too grown to listen to your parents, you feel as if you have no one to talk to, no one can relate to your story. I want to reach out to you rape victims, who are scared to speak out or get any help for yourselves. I want to talk to the depressed men and women, because everyone has a story. I'm not saying mine is worse than any one of you. I just want people to know, what it's like to walk in my shoes. Finally, being able to express myself I picked up a pen and piece of paper, because there once was a time I couldn't express myself all to anyone. Emotionally I would like for you young ladies, girls, boys, women, teens, and any persons! If you may be going through a situation similar to any story in this book, to open your mind and heart as you read through these pages. We all have been victimized and no I'm not talking about the victims! I'm talking about their stories, because they may help save a life, or open your eyes so you can feel pure and alive again. I want to let the runaway, hot, and hard-headed children, know that you are not alone.

We all have been there, but it is hope left within us and it's up to us whether we chose to learn and get stronger from the situation or not, I have faith in Jesus Christ my savior and his father my God! All you have to do Is Reach out to him, keep the faith, confess with your mouth and believe with the heart, let go and let God, because the battle is not ours it's the lord. God didn't bring us this far to leave us and he said he wouldn't put more on us then we can bare, because by his stripes we are covered. A lot of us are crying out for help and no one see the signs! Well I'm here to help so read these stories. Hopefully by the end of this book you will be ready to open up, get help or justice, and step up to the things you couldn't before. You were too scared to tell the police, and your parents! So now you're suffering from depression, wondering why it happened to you. Let me reach out to comfort and let you know everything will be ok. I'll

be the voice to help get you justice, or speak up for you because it's
hard and you don't want to live your whole life in the past. Just because you fear people judging you, please don't be afraid or give up! If you do, then you're only giving them (or it) the power over you and your life. Let's stand together and make our voices rise to be heard. I love each and every one of you, may God bless you....

Thanks for reading,

Lakyshia L (Shelton) Hubert

Table of Contents

Prologue:

Where to start I can finally open up!

Keisha and her family moved to Harlem Florida, where I met a girl named Candice Wisdom which would end up being very close to me! Candice and I went to school together! A few years went by and Candice would tell me that she's so angry with me because I kept everything inside! A few more years pass by and we became best friends! We've fought, and argued, etc. But our friendship grew and was never broken. I wondered how could it be and we were next door neighbors all in all. I said to her one day, how could I have met a friend like you? That's so true, and never once have anything I told you went anywhere except from me to you? Candice just smiled and said because I'm your best friend and that how we will remain, because friends do not tell friends business! My family and I have moved over the years back and forth from town to town. A lot of things just seemed to be going wrong in my life. It was as if everything I touched got messed up. I don't have any one to tell "I'll say to myself" then one day while living in Fort Myers Florida, I met this guy, (short, dark chocolate, average weight) named Jack. Oh my! When I laid eyes on him my stomach got butterflies. We begin to talk and as the weeks went by, I felt as if I was ready to lose my virginity with Jack. So now at age 13 (after having to leave my first love back in Clewiston, which he would later end up being my baby father) I talked to my sister Tee.

(The Conversation)

Keisha: hey sis! I just wanted to let you know I've been thinking about having sex, and I really think I'm ready to lose my virginity with Jack. We're about the same age and he loves me. I want to tell mama, but I don't know how she going to react!

Tee: girl don't tell mama that, "are you crazy" she's going to kill you, Keisha girl you her baby! But here take these condoms, and whatever you do! Do not tell her you talked to me first.

Keisha: ok I won't, but is it going to hurt? I'm kind of nervous sis! LOL!

Tee: yes, it's going to hurt, especially if y'all do not know what y'all are doing!

Keisha: ok sis thanks I love you I'll see you later, give my niece a kiss for me.

Tee: love you to and I will when she wakes up.

A couple days go by and I tell Jack that I didn't want to lose my virginity to anyone in Clewiston! Because the men aren't any good, and plus everyone sleeping with everyone. I also tell him about the boyfriend Ethan that I was forced to leave behind in Clewiston. We talked more and more! Then one night I called and told Jack it was that time.

(The Conversation)

Keisha: my mama is going out tonight and my brother has my niece with him. I'm going to tell him you are coming over.

Jack replies: ok I'll be over there in about 15minutes.i hang up the phone and run to tell my brother Trigga what the plans are going to be.

Mama: kid's hello y'all hear me talking! Eat, take a bath, and go to bed! I'm about to go out and I don't want nobody in my house

Keisha: yes ma'am

Trigga: yes ma'am

I'm watching through the window as my mama pulls off, then I go outside and call jack's name. So, after my mama was completely out of sight, Jack walks out of the dark from the neighbor's yard. We hug and go inside the house! While jack is talking to Trigga, I go jump in the shower. After I'm done I plug up the radio and turn the lights to dim. I then go get Jack and bring him in my room, but not before reminding my brother to tap the wall, yell, and make some noise or something. If mama comes back to the house! Back inside my room Ginuwine-Role Play is just beginning to play softly. I lay on the bed and we begin to kiss and touch each other. Jack gets on top of me and slowly kisses my lips, and then I look him deeply in the eyes and say, "baby I'm ready"! Jack begins to open the condom and put it on. My body then begins to slightly shiver because I'm nervous and afraid that it's going to hurt like my sister says. He slowly begins to slide his penis into my vagina inch by inch. all types of thoughts begin to run through my head, as I'm starting to relax jack kiss me, but before we could do anything further... The room door opens, and it's my mama. Jack freeze up, lies down and try to play sleep.

Mama: what the hell is going on in here?

(Waits a minute! no response)

Mama: boy if you don't get your ass up out my house within the next 2seconds, I'm going to throw your black ass out that damn window

Jack: (jumps up grabs things) yes ma'am

(Front door closes)

Mama: I ought to beat your ass right now, but I'm going to let your father deal with you when we get to Clewiston.

Keisha: well mama I told tee and Trigga, she said not to tell you

(My mama storms off mad)

Keisha: bro why didn't you tell me mama was coming? I whispered!

Trigga: man, sis when I looked up mama was standing there asking where you were at! So, I told her you were in the room with our niece. She said how cause our niece was in there with me. I forgot, and mama opened your door.

Keisha: o ok whatever I don't know why you said that....

I was 13 when this happened, now at that time of being immature and hardheaded. Experiencing different things, I had to learn the hard way about wanting to rush into adult hood. Little did I know, this was just the beginning of a lifetime of heartache and pain!

Chapter One Pain of Betrayal

Keisha moved back to Clewiston and ran back into Ethan (soon to become baby daddy) things was crazy because after we decided to try and have sex (after all the times of us being together and trying to see each other) he made me bleed when we did so it, and boy did it hurt so bad. Ethan says to me, I thought you said that you weren't a virgin anymore! I replied baby I told you what happened, and that I was not sure because I got caught. Ethan says well obviously he did not do his job because it looks like your cherry just popped. A few years pass by (I had a son with another dude) and we meet up again after being in and out of an on &off relationship, when Ethan shows up at my job! Soon as our eyes touched it was like a breath of cold air, where you could feel the burning sensation that we had for one another. We talked a little trash to each other and he left but came right back. So, then I go on lunch break where we talked for a while, then he looked me deeply in the eyes and said what do you want to say to me? I replied Ethan I'm still in love with you (I said as I turned my head). Why are you looking away? Asks Ethan! I again reply because I don't like rejection! Ethan says well I have something to tell you also, look at me! I looked at him, when suddenly he just gently grabbed my head and pulled me over then kissed me so passionately. Ethan then says I still love you to! I then go back into work smiling because I'm happy, and he left (at least I thought)! Later that night when I got off work he's sitting outside and yells I know you thought I was gone but I waited to see if you may have needed a ride home! back at the house we chill and he ends up falling asleep, then one year after that things started falling apart (I mean between the arguments with his mama, sisters, ex-girlfriends, sideline girlfriends, secret girlfriends, whatever you want to call them) but we loved each other so much until were willing to deal with pretty much anything. I mean he cheated with this fat bitch uptown, and then another one who would later try to spread lies. So, I then moved back to Fort Myers and slept with this guy which wanted to talk to me awhile back. All in all, Ethan knew all of what was going on with me because he would come over with my brother Trigga to get a little cash etc... So, over the three years we were back together things went up and down.

That's when one day I got tired of it all and met this young man (whom I just basically later used to get away from Ethan). One-night Ethan and I got into an argument on the phone and he tell me bitch you would never leave me because you love me too much. "That was the last and final straw! The next day I called Ethan and told him that I was going to have sex with dude (whom I'm going to just call Virgo)! Now from then on, it was more arguments and drama anything you can name because I was still sleeping with Ethan! A short while later I find out I'm six weeks pregnant!! But I had only been talking to Virgo about one month and we did not have sex until about two weeks after us meeting (just being honest, I even told Virgo not to sign my baby birth certificate) so I knew it was not his baby. Now all the way up until I was about four months pregnant Ethan would go with me to all the doctor's appointments, and I'll spend the night with him, he would rub my back, etc.... that's until he got locked up, so now that Ethan was gone (Virgo and I started talking, and was getting more involved with each other) but I was accepting calls from Ethan in the county jail and sending him money, only to find out from his little brother that his ex-girlfriend was also send him money...hell he could've just kept it real with me and let me keep my little money in my pocket, but he actually was trying to play me when I was keeping it real with the both of them. Ethan knew I had his back and would always take him back no matter what! But at the same time, I was starting to build some type of relationship with Virgo, and I also was getting further along in my pregnancy of my second child. Virgo and I rented two rooms in a rooming house, In Moore haven Fl because I was getting close to having the baby. February 22, 2010, I gave birth to a beautiful 7lbs 9ounces baby boy. Around March 17, 2010 I received a phone call from Ethan, saying he's been released from jail.

(The Conversation)

Keisha: hello

Ethan: hey how are you and the baby doing?

Keisha: we're doing fine! We are coming over there, so you can see the baby.

Ethan: ok but I want to ask you are we still doing the DNA test because I know that's my baby.

Keisha: ok well let me talk to Virgo because he is acting like he doesn't want to take it anymore, but anyway I'm going to ask my brother to bring us over there.

Ethan: ok then see you in a little while.

(Phone Hangs Up)

Virgo, my brother Trigga and I, meet up with Ethan and his sister Missy at the Child support office. I go in and speak with the receptionist, and she tells me that I cannot request for the DNA test, that Virgo would have to request for it, but Virgo got mad and said no because that's his baby and he always going to be there for him even if he's not his son. So, we then go back to Ethan mother house, and they're taking pictures of the baby with Ethan when his mother bust out this is my grandson. I asked what did you say ma? This is my grandson she repeats. We leave and head home to Moore haven. Virgo and I argued and argued over the next two weeks, and then he hit me and knocked my gold tooth out. He also split my left eyebrow towards the end and made me sprang my ankle. That's when Ethan stepped up and moved in with me and our baby (he was there a couple weeks maybe), but the whole time we were there having sex or whatever, Virgo was peeking in the window watching us. Virgo would come over and bring me beer (Natural Ice is what I prefer), and marijuana for me and Ethan to smoke. Virgo would then get mad when I tell him I didn't want to get back with him, and then try to hit me. I'll scream, Ethan comes out and Virgo takes off running. I ended up having to go back to the hospital for them to check my ankle, Ethan has the baby (or so I thought), but I'll later find out he let another chick hold my son. We get back home from the hospital and still end up having it out with Virgo and some people from the town (who we all know and chilled with at some point)! Now it's time for me to go sing with the choir and I find out about this nothing ass round the way Labelle foot dragging b***h saying Ethan is her man, so we bump heads and argued, then I told her hold up I'm on my way over there and Ethan is going to be with me and our child.. we have a few more words and I hang up the phone. we head to church and after it's over I go outside before church let all the way out, that's when my sister in law say, sis these hoes talking about jumping me! I'm like whom? but before she could answer this impala pulled up and all the doors opened, so many chicks came out and started fighting my sister in law, Ethan throwing chicks and pushing them to the ground, and this tall chick was jumping in the fight I hit her ass one time and she dropped. Now everyone from inside the church is outside the fight breaks up quickly, now the chick I was posed to fight is sitting on the park laughing. Then she calls Ethan mom and say I let her get jumped. The whole while you posed to be Ethan ole' lady, so why you didn't come help your sister-in-law fight? Matter of fact you called your home girls and told them your sister-in-law was trying to

19

holler at their man, and sent them at her, not me! But that's your in law, right? later that night she calls Ethan sister and I get on the phone, she say's o yea that night you were in the hospital and Ethan had your baby, and he was with your dad! Yeah, I say! She says I held your baby, and the next time you come to church over here I'll hit you in your shit while you are holding your baby. I snapped! Some months go by I get back with Virgo and Ethan start dating some girl, but I was still going over there staying with him. They eventually end up breaking up sometime later, but I'm still getting motel rooms and staying whenever I could with him. Around October 3, 2010 I go to my mother house and my 11-year-old niece Nisha (at the time) say's auntie, I have something I really need to tell you! I reply what's up boo, gone and tell me whatever you got to say cause I'm about to go. My niece replies it's about Uncle Ethan and Cousin Beth! I stop quickly and say what? Tell me now!

Well auntie.... She pauses! Uncle Trigga and Uncle Ethan went to pick up Cousin Beth, brought her and her little sister Amy over here. We were supposed to go to aunt Mona house and get in the pool, but when they got here (she continues) they were all in the room hugging and kissing. They wouldn't let us in until granddad made them open the door. I say wait hold up auntie baby let me get this straight! Ethan and Beth were in my mother house hugged up, and kissing? Well hold up, I left Ethan with my kids, so where the hell were they? (I asked in a mad tone) Auntie, she replies he had them. I say o hell no! (Now my sister Tee is like I told her she is not wrong for telling you)! I dial Ethan number it goes straight to voicemail, so then I dial Beth number! Phone rings.... Rings again... Then she answered hello! I said so cousin you sleeping with my baby daddy? Y'all were hugged all up and kissing in my mama house over my kids? Beth replies cousin what you talking about? I say bitch when was you going to tell me you fucking my baby daddy? Don't play dumb! She replies bitch I didn't fuck him yet, but I am soon then hung up. I then called my brother Trigga and said, so you mean to tell me that you going to take Ethan to be with Beth, and bring them to mama house over my kids disrespecting shit? He then says nothing! Hello, I say! He responds yes sister! I then say there's no way in the world you could tell me you didn't know what was going on! You are supposed to be my brother and this how you do me your blood sister, baby sister at that. I tell you what then after mom and dad renew their vows don't you ever talk to me again just act like I'm not your sister and you don't even know me. So, over the next couple weeks (from that 3rd day in October till around the 16th when I found out Beth had moved in with Ethan and his mom) it was so much arguing, commotion, and drama. I'm crying my eyes out constantly and Virgo is like wow I don't believe he would do something like that after all the time y'all known each other! I respond and say, I don't know why they didn't get together back in the day when we were growing up! Why wait until now to do this! (But tells Beth that he wrote her letters before she came home, but I didn't send them which was a lie He knew he only wrote her one time when we were together on a letter I sent her, when I sent her pictures of my oldest son.) Everyone was talking about me, and telling me why are you crying? (It doesn't matter anyway isn't the other dude (Virgo) your baby daddy who signed for your baby) Ethan family was talking about me, picking, wanting to fight, and drag my name through the dirt. I'm home alone at night looking at my baby boy, (which looks just like his family) crying, and crying. Nobody to talk to and stressed out, because no matter what we went through I loved that man throughout anything! Even though I was hurting, my heart still longed for his love, and I couldn't just stop loving him. (I had not seen him since earlier the day that everything first started) then I finds out he told my dad that the baby was not his son. That was it! I called this reality show (that does DNA test and a lot of people watch it all across the world), I told them my story and that I really need a DNA test cause my ex signed my son birth certificate after I told him it wasn't his baby, and now he refusing to do one. I went on to explain on how Ethan was a great dad to his son, and my older son until the day I found out about him and my cousin Beth. So, they flew us to Stamford Connecticut November 2, 2010 and gave us the DNA test results on November 3, 2010: Ethan you are the father. Then it was even more drama and more drama until I felt like there was nothing left of me. I felt like how this man could come and build up my self-esteem all these years and be the one to turn around and tear it down! The pain of betrayal that I felt was unbelievable and now it's to the point of hate and wanting to commit a crime of passion. I'm trying to work things out in my head, while listening to Mary j. Blige- missing you, all day and night! Crying over and over whenever I was alone, Ethan insists on telling our son to call Beth mama. How do you get over so much pain? Will I lose my mind, or will I hold on and maintain? Trust me it was hard and the thought about moving on was driving me insane, because we usually end up back together. this time it won't happen, I had to make myself be strong and realize this man has no respect for me at all, or he wouldn't have done that from the start whether we were together or not. He knew that was his son, and she was my cousin (Blood or not)! So even if I wanted him back and still loved him, I knew it would never be me and Ethan again. I left to another state just to get away and find myself over again. Now it's an emergency with my best friend and I rush back home to Florida. It's been five months since all of this started, and I've had to stay humbled, bite my tongue, and walk away from a lot. I was bitter and mad with all men, thinking all them were dogs, mad at the world (because he could've slept with anyone else besides someone close to me or my family). I was done with love; Ethan made me hate all men, and that's when I met up with Jam. O my he swept me off my feet and captivated me by his words and gentle, yet firm touch. I explained to him all my pain and he assured me that I no longer had to worry. I was bitter and didn't believe him, and then around April 8, 2011, we made it official that we were a couple and at that very moment he helped mend my heart. He showed me how to love again; he treats me like a queen and respects me as a lady. Now it's January 2013, and our wedding is next month February 16,

2013! I can truly and happily say I'm in love. Thank God for the experience because it made me a stronger woman and prepared me for this awesome man, whom hand I'm about to accept in marriage. I forgave Ethan and Beth a long time ago not for them but for myself. thank you for taking time out to read my personal story, hurtful yet emotional but I'm thankful because the woman I am today, is better than the woman I was before and that's because I'm walking by faith. I wake up smile and thank God for blessing me and never giving up on me. I had to take it one day at a time because Ethan also told Beth that I still wanted him and was texting him.

It's a good thing Jam had my phone and seen where Ethan texted me and said that he would fight over me, and a whole lot of other mess. He also tells people that he just ran over me and always cheated on me and told me in my face, but why argue when I know none of that is true... obviously it was something that kept us together back then and if you going to tell something tell it how it is. We all slept on the floor, what black person hasn't made a pallet? I have nothing to hide no one is perfect, but if you're going to do something be man or woman enough to own up to it. The decisions you make today is going to reflect on you tomorrow. I tried to make plans and let Ethan be a part of our son life, but Beth tells someone that he jacks my son up and throw his against the bed at the age of 1 ½ almost 2 years, and say you going to be nothing but a pussy ass nigga like your step dad Jam. When I tell you it was so much drama, (I regret now my actions because I should have just called the police and let them sort it out) I snapped and was ready to fight because this is my baby, our baby and I felt like Ethan hated me so much that he would do something like this to his own son all because he wanted Beth to take him.... My lord if I would have stayed calm and handled it the right way something could have been done, but once again at the age of 3, I let my son go back over there with his father, now since him and Beth is no longer dating when his mom gets mad with him because he was about to fight her husband. She takes it out on my son and wants him to leave now! The way I feel is it doesn't matter is she living off a fixed income, because she didn't make a baby with me. Ethan should be able to have our son where ever he's at because that's his son also. her income does not have anything to do with me and his son because I lived off a fixed income and take care of my kids, so why he couldn't do it one summer! Ugh it was a mess, but Jam and I is tired of it and ready to stop dealing with them, but we know we can't, then every now and again Virgo pops up to see the baby because his name is still on the birth certificate, even though we have the DNA results.

Chapter two HIV

Anna Marie was a mixed Barbie type of woman with a shape to kill for although she could stun you with her beauty, she had a problem with smoking crack (rock cocaine). Anna Marie would go party with her bisexual best friend Michael, they partied all night long, drinking and smoking...Etc.! The next morning Anna Marie awoke nude and sore. Michael was naked lying right beside her, hey Michael bitch get up and tell me what happened last night! "He replies" Hoe I don't know but where are my clothes? Matter of fact, take those 40$ and go around to J. Buck's house then get something for us to wake up with! Anna Marie walking trying to remember some of the events that had taken place the night before and didn't realize she was in the path of two thirsty brotha's which acted as if they never seen a woman. They were hollering out damn little mama sexy, hope you don't have a man. Anna just kept walking as if she hadn't heard one word they've spoken. The other guy was like o this bitch is too good, then without warning someone grabs Anna from behind and pulls her inside this dead end cut behind the dumpster inside the alley way and covers her mouth. If you scream we will kill you! "Say's one of the men". Anna Marie still tries to fight them off, but the other guy rips all the clothes off and sniff her body scent like a dog. They raped her for what seemed over two hours. They beat her so bad that she couldn't move her body and finally passed out. They made sure before they left to spit on her and kick her several times as they made their exit. So, when Anna Marie awoke 12hours later, she found herself in a hospital bed with an officer inside her room. She groaned as she slowly begins to try and speak.... Wh-wh-wh-what a-a-mm I doing here? She finally managed to get out. the officer looked around in amazement and said Ms. Marie you were raped a short while ago and some people was walking by and heard your cries, they called 911 now you're in the hospital! Let me get the detectives because they want to ask you some questions. Shortly after piecing together with the

officers about the rape incident, the doctor tells her
she need to follow up with her personal doctor.
Anna Marie follows up with the health department
and they draw blood to be sent to the lab for
testing. 2 1/2 weeks later Anna Marie returns home
depressed after being informed that she's pregnant
and it's too early to tell how far along she was, but
to make matters worse the men which raped her
also gave her HIV. Anna Marie was so distraught
and felt as if she had nothing else to live for.
Between smoking, taking medicine for her virus,
and going back and forth to the doctors, Anna
Marie was at the edge. One year later her baby girl
was born already and going on 3months. Anna
Marie phone rings and it's the detectives! Ms. Marie
we're going to need you to come to the station, we
have some information about your case. Sir I'll be
on the way give me 30 minutes or so. When Anna
Marie arrives at the station, she's led into an
interview room where she would later be informed

they have two suspects in custody. Anna Marie was totally crushed because that nightmare was coming back to haunt her. When they did a line, up Anna Marie seen the men but acted as if she couldn't remember what their faces looked like. Shortly after Anna Marie started attending group meetings and going to church to get closer to the lord. Now she was a speaker to new people with her disease that joined the classes. Anna Marie *(H) human (I) Immunode (V) virus

1)   What HIV does- it affects our immune system and then damages it so severely over a period of time. Some viruses, such as the ones that cause a common cold or the flu, only stay in the body a few days.

2)   How to get rid of HIV- some viruses such as HIV will never go away, when a person becomes infected with HIV, that person becomes HIV positive and will always be HIV positive.

3)   What HIV Affects- over time the HIV disease infects and kills white blood cells called cd4 Lymphocytes (or T-cells) and can leave the body unable to fight off certain kinds of infections and cancers.

4)Can HIV Be Transmitted by physical contact-you cannot get HIV just from working with someone who has HIV, sitting on toilet seats, or everyday things like sharing a meal. (Honestly people don't want to take that risk of years later finding out medical research says something different about sharing a meal)

5) What About Being Pregnant, can my child contract it- If a woman has HIV, she can transmit the virus to the child during pregnancy, labour, delivery, or breastfeeding. Without treatment around, 15-30 percent of babies born to HIV-infected women will become infected with HIV during pregnancy, and delivery. Another 5-20 percent will become infected through

breastfeeding. Also, modern drugs are highly effective at preventing mother to child transmission.

Anna Marie says that's all and goes to take a seat, when suddenly a voice spoke up and said Ms. Marie how do you deal with it daily and do you ever feel like giving up?

Anna replies I was beaten and raped by two men, which left me HIV+ and pregnant. My daughter is going on four months, I have to take her back and forth to the doctors to get medicine to try and prevent her from catching the virus. Also, the investigators told me they had a DNA match from the semen they collected and spit from them. Every day is a constant struggle for me. I wasn't going to even pursue going to court but now I have started back going to church and taking these classes are helping me out a lot. I find myself getting sicker and weaker on some days, but I continue to push forward. When I walk off into that courtroom and look them square in the face, I'm going to ask the judge to do a DNA test and see which one fathered my child and for a HIV test on the both of them. I really want to see how they mouth drop wide open.

Chapter Three Aids

Julie Ann was the type of girl every man wanted, she was beautiful caramel, medium build, and slightly tall. Julie Ann hair was always done and she stayed with the newest name brand items that came out. Every time you seen her she was in a fly car with nice rims, music blasting and a pocket full of money. I mean chick had her shit in order, then one hot day Julie Ann was making her usual rounds with her girls when she happen to stumble across her a new client. He was a real smooth dark chocolate silky skin, muscular, tall man. Damn he was fine! On top of that he was spending 1000 dollars! after a couple weeks with her new client Julie Ann found herself walking up and down the strip turning tricks and getting her ass whooped if she didn't have 1000 dollars every Two weeks, and sometimes during the week he would come over and take what she's made so far. Then he tells her she better have his money still by the end of the week. Julie Ann falls to the floor crying, thinking what the hell she got herself into. So, she gets out and round up a couple girls to hit the streets. Julie Ann meets a young girl that's red and very pretty. She's looking so lost, hurt, and confused! So, Julie Ann walks up to her and says 'hey what's up I'm Julie "the girl replies" hey I'm Tasha! Julie ask do you want to make some cash jump on my team; I got some work lined up right now. Tasha say's hell yea let's go I'm game for whatever. They leave and get better acquainted; Julie does Tasha hair and gets a nice, sexy, leg revealing dress. Back to the streets they go, making triple the amount Julie was making before, because now she had a partner and sister. When it was time to pay the allowance, Julie told her guy straight up that she was done, here is your money plus more, if you ever come near me again it's going to be hell in the city. He goes to grab her around the neck, Julie Ann then pulls out her tazor and squeeze down on the button, and she squeeze even harder as he starts dropping to the floor. Julie let the button go, kicks him then kneel down an say listen next time it won't be no tazor, this is your warning don't ever come near me again. Meanwhile Tasha is outside waiting with the car running and trunk open. Julie runs out and throws as much of her stuff inside as they could. Then they jump inside and speed away. The next couple years pass and overtime they would still hit clients up, but then Julie started dating this guy and moved in with him, of course Tasha was there also. Then about 3 months after that Julie told Tasha that her and her friend was moving to Miami. Tasha refused to come along, so they then kind of lost touch for a while. About 6 months and 2 days after Julie moved to Ft. Myers from Miami, she gets a phone call!

Phone rings!

Julie: hello, oh hi mom how you doing?

Mom: baby I just found out some news about your friend Tasha.

Julie Ann: replies ok mama what happened with Tasha now?

Mom says: your friend smokes crack!

Long pause

Julie Ann: replies no ma you can't be talking about my friend, who I used to be with like my shadow.

Mom Says: Julie you know I wouldn't lie!

Julie: ok mom I know, I'll be down there tomorrow!

Phone hangs up!

Julie Ann then grabs a 20 piece of crack and went back to where she had left a while ago. (Julie has never seen that man again) Julie heads to Harlem garden apartment 600 block to find Tasha.

Knock, Knock! Who is it?

Julie! (Door Opens)

Julie sits the 20 on the counter and faces Tasha! I don't believe you smoking crack and I'm not going to believe it until I see it, "says Julie Ann"! Tasha replies no because you going to hit me. No, I'm not yells Julie; I just want to know if it's true! So, Tasha then picks up the crack rock and put it on her pipe and smokes it!

The conversation:

Julie Ann starts crying and asks why?

Tasha: because I lost my son, you moved away, my family turned their backs on me, and I didn't have anybody, so I was over here chilling and Gee & Nicole was smoking. I asked them could I hit it. Now

Julie, she goes on; everyone saying they started me, but it's not true. I was going through something and it's something I chose to do.

Julie Ann: turns to leave but stopped and said all you had to do was call me, because this is not going to help your problem at all its only going to make it worse. Whenever you ready let me know, because I can't help anyone who doesn't want to be helped. A

few years pass by and now Tasha has 3 kids (two girls and one boy) but has no custody of not one of them. Julie Ann has 2 boys (one is with her parents) and Julie has full custody of both her children, it seems that everyone thinks or wanted to think she lost custody. Julie then finds out that Tasha has contracted aids from her youngest child father. So, Julie

asks Tasha one night did she know that her baby father had Aids!? Tasha replies no she didn't know that he was sick. Julie then replied "Tasha" girl that's a charge because he knew he was sick and chose not to tell you, hell no he can go to prison for murder that way, because basically you just lost your life and you having these kids knowing damn well y'all sick that's some fucked up shit dog. You know I'm going to keep it real with you always. Tasha says: sis hold up I did not want to get him in trouble because I knew they was going to lock him up. Then when I was in labour up under that medicine, they asked me if I still wanted my tubes tied

after I already signed the papers and I said no. Julie responded bitch what the fuck, it doesn't matter whether you said no, because you already signed the consent papers. You're tripping jeez! Julie couldn't believe what her ears were hearing. Have her friend lost her fucking mind or is she just plain stupid, def, and dumb. Julie talked with Tasha for a while, and then went to look up on the internet what Aids was, and how it works.

(A) Acquired (I) Immuno (D) Deficiency (S) Syndrome

1) A healthy person usually has a cd4 (white blood cells) count of between 600 and 1200, but when the cd4 count drops below 200, a person immune

system is severely weakened, and that person is then diagnosed with aids even if he/she has not become sick from other infections.

2) How you should think of Aids- you should think of Aids as an advanced HIV disease. persons with Aids has an immune system so weakened by HIV that the person usually becomes sick from several opportunistic infections or cancers such as P.C.P (a type of pneumonia) or K.S (Kaposi sarcoma), wasting syndrome (involuntary weight loss) memory impairment, or tuberculosis (TB). Someone with HIV is diagnosed with one of these opportunistic infections (even if the cd4 count is above 200) he/she is said to have Aids.

3) How long does it take to develop or discover Aids? - Aids usually take time to develop from the time a person acquires HIV usual between 2 to 1015 years.

4) Once a person has been diagnosed with Aids, she/he is always considered to have aids, even if the cd4 count goes up again and/or they recover from the disease that defined their aids diagnosis.

5) After your diagnosis of Aids is made the current average survival time with antiretroviral therapy is estimated to be now more than 5 years but because new treatments continue to be developed and because HIV continues to evolve resistance to treatments, estimates of survival are likely to continue to change antiretroviral medication can prolong the time between the HIV infection and the onset of Aids, without antiretroviral therapy death normally occur within a year. But most patients die from opportunistic infections or malignancies associated with the progressive failure of the immune system.

After reading this Julie Ann told Tasha I'll never treat you differently but you got to stop sleeping with these men knowing you have this disease. Tasha replies: hell, I tell them, and they don't care. Julie says: wow that's so fucked up half of these men know you sick and still sleep with you, on top of that they turn around and go home to their ole lady and sleep with her. Wow I've never seen no one, so down and dirty to just pass that sickness around.

Tip#1) Ladies know who you are sleeping with because it's some dirty people in this world.

Tip#2) Go get tested, and don't let no one say o I'm clean don't you believe me. Still get tested or have them show you their most recent Aids test, but if they refuse then something is wrong.

Tip#3) No matter if no one agrees to go with you or you're scared, go anyway because knowing and doing something about it, instead of not knowing and spreading it from person to person.

Chapter Four Depression

Katie was a dark skinned, average sized woman with curves in all the correct places. Every now and again she would actually wear makeup but other than the club scene times she would only wear lip liner, eye shadow, and lip gloss. She had her very own unique swag, but to most people she was nothing but a black low life chick that no one liked and started to pick on and bullied every day. They started calling her root dog, and even made a little song that goes: root dog...root let them widows up root root let them windows up. On top of that she had this cousin who didn't like her for any apparent reason, and always acted as if she was the shit because she was short with a nice body, red with long hair down her back, which led people to believe she was mixed or something! So, she always looked down on Katie like she's not the one you hear about every week in school that was fighting over a man (different man I should say), every time you turn around, but that wasn't Katie problem! Katie problem started from home being the youngest of the family and her mom was on drugs, married but moved out and got an apartment where her, and her brother met their step-father (well Katie eventually started calling him dad, but her brother Trigga wasn't going for it)! Katie could remember working in the hood store and dealers would come up to her on payday talking about your mom said that when you got paid, you would pay us such & such, because we fronted her this and that. Katie would respond a little pissed and say listen motherfucker when you gave her that shit did I say I was going to pay you? Was I there? This is my fucking money and what I'm making is mine, straight up what the fuck I look like. so, then it started being to where Katie would have to ask grown men at an early age for money just, so her mom could get high or whatever and if she didn't she would get called all types of names. Such as: bitch, hoe, you aren't shit, never going to be shit and nobody would ever want you. Katie was shocked and couldn't get over the embarrassment of being told this in front of everyone on the street. Those things started bothering her so badly, but she continued to hold everything inside. It always seemed that no matter how much Katie tried to fit in, someone always picked on her. it's not that they didn't have nice things, a home, food, a vehicle... etc., it's just Katie was hard on shoes, so her mom decided not to buy her real expensive name brand shoes because all she did was mess them up within a week of getting them. they also would go around and tell people Katie was dirty and didn't bathe, all kinds of thing's when they really didn't know the real Katie or never been inside her house, cause anyone would tell you Katie mother would wake you up 4:00 am if she came home and her kitchen was not cleaned and you better not missed the bus after you done, because if she woke you up and you went back to sleep that's your ass. Also, she would make you get on your knees with a toothbrush and scrub all around the corners and cracks. But people still picked on Katie called her black and ugly, so much that she started feeling depressed with very low self-esteem. By the time Katie got old enough to seek help through mental health it was too late because the damage was done. They tried giving Katie Cymbalta and Prozac for depression they had to prescribe sleeping pills for Katie because she couldn't seem to fall asleep at night, her weight would go up and down. She was just stressed, then every time she would be ok with no pills etc. Then all over again she would break down and go back into that depressive stage now she tries to stay prayed up and taking things one day at a time.

Chapter Five Wanting to Commit Suicide

Have you ever been under so much stress and then you get more bad news from your family about someone you love, that tares you up on the inside and make you feel like you're worth nothing at all and never meant anything to that person at all. Well here is my story!

I'm Keshondra and I've made mistakes in my life, but always kept it real with the man I loved named Kory. So, it's about time for me to go to court because I'm just going to take the six months in the county jail. October 1, 2008 comes, and the judge tries to talk me into just taking the plea offer, 1-year drug offender probation with 2 years driver license suspended, and random drug screening. I refused because I'd rather take 6months county time and get it all over with. So, I give Kory a hug, and tell him I love him as I'm being taken into custody. I'm mad at nobody but myself! So, a month passes, and my brother brings Kory to come see me, so I asked him was there anything he needed to tell me? He said no! So, the next week come and this time they bring my son with them, but its two skinny chicks whom I assume is with them because they we're lounging around the visiting screen. So, I asked Kory again was there anything he wanted to tell me because a man going to do what a man want to do, hell I'm locked up and I know you're not going to wait for me to get out. All I'm asking you is to keep it straight up and real with me, I can handle the truth. Kory replies no baby I would never do anything like that to hurt you after all these years and everything we been through just to be together, I wouldn't jeopardize that for one of these stank ass girls. I love you Kesh baby do you believe me because you know there is not one thing I wouldn't do just to see you smile ok baby. I reply yes baby I hear you, would I see y'all next week? Yes, ok bye. A few weeks go by then Keshondra gets a visit and it's her mother this time, wow what's really going on I begin to think to myself. I pick up the little phone receiver and the monitor pops on, I say hello mother how are you today? What's going on?

Mom say: well baby girl I thought I'll come deliver the news myself. Kory wet to jail a couple days ago, and I asked him, and your brother did they have some weed on them and that I didn't want that in my truck (we had a white four door Silverado truck with a DVD player inside, and we lived at a corner apartment). My mom continued to say I had a feeling they was hiding something because they kept going inside that empty apartment next door and coming in all hours of the night.

I say: what ma are you serious? So, what was he arrested for?

My mother responded: saying they was riding around late and got pulled over for suspicious activity, when they got ready to search the truck Kory told him where the weed was at, and that nobody else in the truck knew about it.

I replied: wait! Was someone else in the truck with them mom?

Yes, she replies: 'the girl was from Belle Glade or somewhere and she was 16 years old, but they tried to lie and say she was 18 years old. I try to hold it together until after my mother left, and then I called home to speak with my brother Trigga and obtain his side of the story.

Phone picks up!

You have a collect call from Keshondra, to accept this call press one now! Beep!

I hear my brother on the line, so I say what's up bro? Mama came and visited me and told me Kory went to jail and y'all had a 16-year-old chick with y'all! What's that about, because the last time I checked you was my brother, and you don't take your brother law to cheat on me especially with an 16year old, damn y'all couldn't find no one 18 years or older? Long pause hello I know you hear me! I said!

My brother Trigga replies: well that's my brother and I'll never leave him, because he wouldn't leave me.

So, I yelled through the phone: are you fucking serious I'm your baby sister what the hell you mean? I'm pissed off now because he has nothing more to say.

So, I hang up and I walk to my bunk crying and stressed feeling like I just wanted to die right then and there. How could this man lie to me and hurt me so bad! That's when mental health comes to visit me and I'm not in such a good pleasant mood, I snapped because the lady keeps asking me the same dumb behind question and it was really making me madder and madder, so I started snatching back on my hair pulling some out yelling I would whoop your ass. I mean I just wanted to roll over and die! She just smiled and said I'm a have you brought down to medical. Next thing I know I'm on suicide watch for seven days. That was the worse feeling in the world having people stare at you all day and not give you any cover, or spoon to eat with. I had to break the side of my styrophone plate and scoop your food up with that. I really felt like just ending it all right there and then. So, after I got out me and Kory was writing each other, he was basically explaining himself. I ended up taking him back,(before I received his letter which stated mama always told me you ain't got no friends to never trust a bitch, you sitting in jail and they're free on the street, and that he change his hoes like he change his drawls) he apologized and said I took it the wrong way. Then after we moved to Moore Haven Fl, I find his police report it goes on to say something like this:

Officer: I observed a white vehicle circling the block, so I then performed a traffic stop. When asked if I could search the vehicle Mr. Kory said sir the marijuana you find is all mine, they had no knowledge I had that on me.

Officer: so, sir you are telling me everything I find is your only

Kory: yes sir

Officer: we then called the minor mother to come pick her up after finding over 20grams, and a rolled-up marijuana cigarette. I then asked Mr. Kory why he had the drugs.

Kory: my girlfriend Keshondra just got arrested, and we just had a baby. Christmas coming up I had to start back selling drugs to support them.

I was like are you seriously going to use me and my child, especially when I turned myself in October 2008, and he didn't get locked up until a couple days before Christmas and you going to disrespect me like that. Hell, no I was fed up and started falling back into that depressive suicide stage then I had this fat hood rat chick in Hooterville wanting to spread lies and stuff. I was done and when I decided to pour all them pills in my hand wanting to take every single one of them, then a little voice said to me Kesh what's wrong with you have you lost your mind! You didn't overcome what you went through to take your life about a man, what about your son? Did you stop to think about him! That's when Kory had the nerve to buss out and say o you would never leave me because you love me. I mean just talking mad shit; I sucked them tears up, threw them pills away, looked him dead in the eyes and said it's over man. Yes, I love you and all, but don't you ever tell me that I won't leave you. I put up with you and all your shit because I loved you not because you are the only person I can or cannot get. Shortly after I found out that I was pregnant with a baby boy and was still seeing Kory, but through all the pain I realized my life is worth more then what you may think and before I hurt myself over a man,

I'll rather just go and be by myself. I was real young, but God is father and Jesus is the key to him, without him I wouldn't be able to tell you this story.

Chapter Six Walking Alone

Keisha kept getting into trouble in school; she was hot headed and never took any mess. So, one day Keisha and this girl get into a fight because the girl was talking about Keisha mother. They got sent to a development academy, where you had to earn rank in order to return to regular school. It was almost as if you were in boot camp or something. So, on her first day at the new school Keisha met up with an old friend name Diane, and the girl she fought Kira. Everything started off good, but by the time they ended up in 10th grade, it was this boy in the class named VJ, and he was short decent looking, but super aggravating. he just had to be the class clown, and one day Keisha walks into class and Diane says girl you got to watch out for VJ, he is very nasty and he would also touch you, then when you tell him to stop he gets mad and cuss you out and act like he's madder then you are. Keisha responds and says no you can't be serious? What does the teacher say when y'all tell him, that's when Kira said 'girl the teacher be looking, but act like he doesn't see anything? Well thank you for telling me that because my mom said you tell a person three times and if they don't do nothing about it, then you handle it yourself. So, the first time VJ tried Keisha, she had just walked in class and took her seat, when he took a seat next to her, and grabbed my hand and said hey feel this. That's when he shoved my hand in his pocket, it felt hard. Oh my gosh it was his penis! I quickly grabbed my hand out of his pocket and was like get the fuck away from me, straight up I don't play them type of games, get away from me. So, over the next week or so VJ would either wait until girls stood up and walk behind them and rub his stuff against you. Now Keisha was pissed off and ready to fight because there was no way the teacher couldn't see what was going on in his classroom. Keisha was fed up with all this foolishness because she went to school to learn and not be sexually harassed, and she felt like she was walking alone. Keisha then went to the principal, but he sent her back to class. When VJ did it again Keisha went back to the principal the second time, he was busy, so she got sent back to class. Now on the third occasion VJ was still at the same old tricks messing with all the girls so Keisha had enough she went back to the principal office one last and final time. This time when she was told to leave she said ok my mama told me to warn y'all three times and if nothing was done about it to handle it myself. So, Keisha goes back to class and VJ goes to grab her, that's when she slapped his hand and snapped. Don't put your fucking hands on me I'm tired of this, that's when the teacher calls the principal because Keisha is pissed and going off, so she gets in trouble because there was no calming her down. Now back at the principal office he informs her that if you fight there you get sent to the program. Keisha calls her dad because she knew she was telling the principal like her mom said and nothing was being done. They wouldn't even change his or her class. Keisha was walking alone until her, Diane, and Kira got together and pressed charges, but even after they did that, they still wouldn't change their classes. Keisha dad withdrew her out of school, now eventually he was arrested, but Keisha still to this day does not know what happened with the case, but she does know he was on the streets a few days later. She felt as if she was walking alone, why she had to give up going to school, to now be later in life struggling trying to make a brighter future for herself and her children. She won't give up, she's aiming for getting her GED and going back to school, so she would be able to prove to herself that even a high school dropout can do it! the moral to the story is when you feel as if you're walking alone all you have to do is think about your role model, or someone you look up to and think if they can do it so can you.

Whatever you put your mind to anything is possible.

Chapter Seven: Abuse

What is abuse, said the teacher! Nobody knows, well your assignment for this weekend is abuse! Whether it's mental, physical, or emotional abuse is abuse. I want y'all to write me a one or two-page story about abuse. Class dismissed!

Rose was a quiet laid back, medium to average build, dark skinned sista, with short hair. Now she had friends because her style, the way she talked and didn't take any shit from nobody at all. But you really just had to push, strike, or just keep picking at rose for her to fight. Back home she had an older sister named Tina. Now over the years Tina has had her picks in men. Tina had a little girl and eventually moved to another town where she met her current scumbag boyfriend named Sean. now when you first meet Sean and he's not drinking alcohol you wouldn't think it's the person which I'm about to describe. It's a shame when he has plenty of sense and come from a good home. Now every family has problems and messed up in some kind of way. Sean had been to jail over and over. He could cook a great meal and lord knows he could clean. My sister gets abused by this man and on top of that he tries everybody in the family of his girlfriend, my sister. Rose says she remember when she first met Sean, she didn't like him cause soon as that beer hit his mouth he is talking all sideways and getting slick. Sean had the nerves to tell Rose another sister from California that all she had to do was ask Rose because she done had him before. It was a big argument; a couple months go by and rose is dating this girl named Tosha (a stud) and Rose receive a phone call from Tosha saying her and Sean just got done fighting. Rose says what? Tosha goes on to say I was waiting for you to get home and that bastard tried to rape me, so I punched him in the face and we got to fighting, but your sister didn't say anything. The next incident happened at night about them arguing and then he kicked Rose sister in the mouth. The next issue my cousin was living with Rose sister Tina for a month or two, and one night Sean called his self-getting her high on powder and drunk all up so she can fall asleep and when she did, he tries (but Rose honestly feel like they had sex) to sleep with her on the bed next to rose sister then one day he wanted to have sex with Tina and she wasn't in the mood, so he gets mad and start throwing all the food he bought for the house out. Then he took a brick and tried to bust her head, luckily, she got away. Sean also was caught naked inside my sister house with another man but say's nothing was going on after he had done already said that he would do a man in the butt if it's about that cash. The point of the story is all in the end rose sister ended up leaving her home, had the lights disconnected and supposingily their relationship is over, for now anyway. but if you know anyone who is getting abused in any way, shape, or form urge them to get out if they can, if not urge them to get help, or talk to someone before one of them blows hits the wrong way and that kills her. Rose and her family still fears if Sean talks to her sister Tina, that he will talk her into coming back and that he's eventually going to kill her.

Rose teacher was shocked at this amazing story she wrote and gave her an a+ for her assignment, she also asked her after class was over to stay behind because she really needed to speak with her.

Chapter Eight:

Rape

(The First Half)

Foxie was new to the neighborhood, and she started going to Alva middle school where she met Noell, he was slim, tall, and dark skinned. They started dating; he would come over to her house and hang out on a daily basis. The beginning of their relationship everything was fine, and they were getting along just fine. Foxie had done lost her virginity a short while earlier, but gotten caught by her mother, so she was no longer allowed to speak to that guy or have him inside the house. So, you understand that what Foxie is about to explain came as a surprise after she found out. Now Noell was at Foxie house and that's when she met Leon which she would later find out are her first (to take her virginity) brother, and Noell cousin. So Foxie mom told them they could spend the night for what reason she does not know, but she does know that when her and Noell went to chill in her room and was about to get into the mood when Leon opened the door walked in and sat on the floor. Foxie yelled get out my room. Noell says baby don't worry about him, and she's like hell no, he got to go. That's when Noell jumps on top of her and say Ima get this pussy right now, and I don't care what you say. So, she just lays there uncomfortable while he's pumping in and out of her. Tears start falling and she just wishes it was over. That's when he got off after he was finished before she could move Leon was on top of her. Foxie started screaming no, no, no get off me, stop and he acted as if he did not hear her and made his way inside her. Placed his hands over her mouth and said shut up bitch. Foxie still crying saying no get off me and looks over at Noell, which is just sitting there like nothing is happening to his girlfriend whom he says he love. Those minutes felt like the longest hours of her life, and all she can think is how could this man just sit there while his cousin basically rape her. Foxie was wondering if her brother or mother couldn't hear her cries and plea's, and why wasn't anyone coming to her rescue. After they were finished they got dressed and left. Foxie just laid on the floor crying until she was able to pull herself up and go to the bathroom to take a shower. She was too scared and at the time she didn't really know whether it was considered rape or not. About a month of avoiding Noell, Foxie finally told her brother what happened, and he got pissed. She also told a couple other people who told her she was lying, and nobody would believe her. So, her cousin came from Arkansas and was at her mother house when Noell rode up and jumped off the bicycle!!! Hey Foxie, what the hell going on, why have you been ignoring me? Huh! Foxie replies please leave because I don't want to talk to you no more and he slaps her. But just as he slaps her, her cousin bends the corner and was like o hell no Foxie you better hit his ass back, because we don't play shit around here. Noell jumps back on the bike and head towards our white homies house around the corner. So Foxie, her brother and cousin go around the corner to where he went to confront him about slapping Foxie. When they got there an argument broke out and Foxie slapped Noell back. That's when Noell pulled out this big pocket knife that had six spaces on both sides of the blade part and punched my brother. So, my cousin hit him, and they went to fighting and Noell rode home and came back with his sisters and mother. by this time Foxie mother was there and when Noell along with his family pulled up Foxie mom told them y'all touch my baby all y'all going to die today, I'm telling you a leaf couldn't fall and hit my house because Ima come around there and burn that trailer down to the ground. that's when the police pulled up to try to gain control but Foxie was still too scared and thought nobody would believe her if she had told about the rape incident.

Second Half

Kelly was 2months pregnant and moved to another town, so when it was time for her doctor appointment she would have to catch someone going towards Clewiston or pay someone to drop her off where she would meet up with her baby father. He would go to every doctor visit and breastfeeding class. I mean he was really showing that he wanted to be a part of a family. Than a month passes by and it's time for the next appointment everything goes well, but just as Kelly was about to leave her baby daddy wanted to have sex. Kelly said no not right now because she had been bleeding lightly and the doctor wanted her to not be stressed out, and to get plenty of rest. Baby daddy said what girl you better stop playing with me, as he closed and locked the bedroom door. Kelly says man I don't want no sex, and I'm not playing with you! Baby daddy laid her back on the bed and says you seriously don't want any dick? Kelly says no! What you finna take it? Baby daddy replies hell I don't have to take it, because it's already mine. So, they have sex and all Kelly could think about was after all that she had been through she would have to turn around and deal with another similar situation to what she's already experienced, and on top of that she was pregnant with their baby. About 20 minutes pass and finally he catches his nut then says, that's all my baby needed was some milk from his daddy.

Kelly drags herself up and gets ready to walk out the room, when he grabs her and say what's wrong with you, why you acting like you have an attitude? Kelly says nothing; I need to use the bathroom before I go because my dad is blowing the horn for me to come. Baby daddy says ok Ima walk you outside when you done in the bathroom. Kelly uses the restroom and is now bleeding a little heavier and it makes her scared. Baby daddy walks her out and gives her another kiss, and says ok bae let me know if you're coming back out here. Kelly say ok whatever and tell her dad to pull off. While in the way home her dad looks and says what's wrong with you, why are you looking mad baby girl? Kelly replies nothing dad, I'm just ready to be back home. Later that day Kelly notices she's still bleeding, so she calls the ambulance and goes to the emergency room, where she told them everything that happened except the part about what her baby father did, because one part of her says Kelly it's rape, but the other part saying no it's not rape. How can it be because you're pregnant from him? You say you love him, so how you going to say rape. Kelly was going back and forth with herself, but then the doctor walked in, and says ma'am go home and get plenty of rest. Try not to stress because if you continue to bleed we're going to have to place you in the hospital on bed rest, because you could also have a miscarriage due to you loosing blood. back home everyone would ask if she was ok or not and she would just be like yes. The whole time thinking about that day, she forgave her baby father, and continued to see and be with him, never spoke about it to no one until now. Kelly says she doesn't know how things will go from here but she's tired of beating herself up about it. she wants you all out there reading these pages to know if you're getting hurt, raped, sexual harassed, abused, depressed, low self-esteem, or whatever you may be dealing with to seek help! If you want to remain anonymous, or you scared someone may see you trying to get out and they are going to tell on you, here is what you do please:

1) Try going to a nearby city abuse center

2) Get a toll-free number and call to explain your situation

3) Have someone trust worthy take you somewhere to receive help

4) Go to local sheriff department and file a report
5) Go to the library and research local help centers.

Kelly urges you to seek any type of help please because you never know when the abuse or rape may end up in murder. These stories may help people understand the different kinds of abuse and/or rape in which some may not believe it is, but no means no in any language and stop means stop. No one deserve to be abused or raped, we must rise up and stand together for ourselves and children because if we don't then who will.

Chapter Nine Gonorrhea

Micki and Jerry were the type of people who didn't know whether they wanted to be together or not. They would always go back and forth, growing up. Micki would never be sexually active with Jerry, because she just wasn't ready for all of that. That soon changed after Micki given birth to her son, then got her own place (that her sister left her). Micki cousins Ruby and J.J started dating, then moved in with Micki. Jerry came over one day, and that was all it took to light the spark which never stopped sparkling for one another. Micki and Jerry were seeming to get a bit more serious this time around, then Micki invited her two Spanish friends over to the house, when suddenly Jerry started acting all funny like he wasn't with Micki, Sitting inside her crib at that. So, Micki got pissed off and made everyone leave and that's the last time Jerry or J.J was seen until a week later. Rudy and Mick had to walk all the way to the hood just to find them hanging out at the store! Rudy and J.J goes to fighting, until J.J ran off and disappeared. Later that night Micki and Jerry made up after he tells her that he loves her and wanted her to be the mother of his children. They had protected sex that night, Micki wakes up the next morning to find Jerry gone. Three days pass by and no sign of jerry! So Micki called a guy friend and he told her: if you really want to know if he loves you all you have to do is get a guy you know you wouldn't fuck and wait good until you know he coming home and start making noises like you fucking... Trust me you going to find out, now beware I told one of my home girls to try that and she did but her dude whooped her ass.... But if he doesn't react like that then he doesn't give a fuck about you. Then Micki decide to try that with a friend to see what Jerry reaction was going to be. When jerry walked inside the house and seen Micki on top of dude making sex noises, all he could do is run inside the room to where J.J and ruby was to tell them what was going on. Jerry leaves and returns the next night, but when he comes in the house you could tell something was wrong. He went straight into the bathroom and made a bath, then fell asleep all night inside the tub. The next morning everyone woke up but was being so secretive about stuff. Then Jerry called his mom talking about going to the hospital for a shot of penicillin because he knows something is wrong, and that his penis was hurting him when he pee. Rudy later told Micki that Jerry was trying to say that she gave him a STD. Micki yells o hell no... What Rudy cousin every time we had sex we used a condom. Rudy respond cousin he saying you gave him a STD, but if you say y'all using condoms then I don't see how it was you, unless he's been sleeping with someone else! O yeah, he had said that he wanted to have a baby with you, so he may have taken the condom off because we all know you said you weren't having a baby from him! Micki responds and say I know when we had sex, he had the condom on, so maybe when it slipped out or something he took it off, anyway I'm calling my brother, so he can take me to the doctor. A short while later Micki arrives at the doctor office and explains all the previous events that had taken place. The doctor does the STD test and says if he had to get a shot of penicillin that means he gave it to you because you're not having the symptoms yet. See if you would have given him the STD, you'd be having some type of symptoms by now. The doctor then gives Micki medication for Gonorrhea and tells her to check back in two weeks for a re-test to make sure everything is negative. Micki says that could have easily been HIV, or Aids!

Things you should know about Gonorrhea:

1) Gonorrhea affects the eyes, anus, mouth, genitals, and throat.

2) Gonorrhea can be transmitted via fluids even if a man does not ejaculate.

3) Also, bacterium caused from Gonorrhea can grow in the eyes, mouth, throat, and anus.

4) Gonorrhea can impact the ability to have kids if left untreated.

5) Gonorrhea is caused by bacterium.

6) Gonorrhea can grow easily in the warmth area of the reproductive tact, including the cervix, uterus, and fallopian tubes of women and the Urethra canal in men and women.

7) The majority of women have no symptoms

8) Gonorrhea symptoms in men and women- Discharge, itching, soreness, bleeding, and painful vowel movement.

9) Gonorrhea symptoms in women- pain or burning when you pee, increased vaginal discharge, and vaginal bleeding between periods.

10) Gonorrhea symptoms for men- burning with pee, discharge from penis, painful or swollen testicals.

Complications of Gonorrhea:

If left untreated, Gonorrhea can cause serious and permanent health problems in both men and women.

In women- Gonorrhea can spread to the Uterus or fallopian tube and cause pelvic inflammatory disease (PID). Symptoms maybe mild or even can include pain and fever. PID can lead to internal abscesses (puss filled pockets that are hard to cure) and chronic pain. PID can cause so much damage until women will be unable to have children.

In men- Gonorrhea can cause a painful condition called Epididymitis in tubes attached to the testicals. In rare cases, this may prevent a man from being able to father children. If left untreated Gonorrhea can spread through the blood to joints, this could be life threatening.

Please this is no joke safe sex is the best sex!

Conclusion: Words from The Author

Lakyshia the Author says: I wrote this novel to reach out to the young generation coming up. I want everyone to know that I really do understand what you may be going through (even if I didn't personally experience your particular situation), I have family members, friends, enemies and fake friends also that I have witnessed in situations as such. Also, I want to start a website where no matter if you're in Florida or California, you can still log on and send a message about your situation and you will get the necessary information and help you need to try and remove yourself from the abusive situation. Even if your lost and need a little guidance because I've walked in them shoe's. One thing I want my readers to know that it does not matter if you're black, white, orange, purple, or blue! Male, Female, Tranny, Lesbian Etc... No matter what you are because it's not about the person it's all about the situation and helping them get out. In the beginning of this novel I told y'all I was getting married and February 2013 I did. I begin to write this novel, but it was really hard and very challenging for me, and I was tempted to quit with every line, and chapter I wrote. But thanks to my not husband, he continued to push me forward and motivate me to not give up on my dream of writing. he told me so what baby if people don't like what you tell about everything you experienced watching people close to you abused, and end up sick, dying, or with aids... He told me if I feel that I can help someone or even help myself by expressing the things I've seen, then go for it, because no one else seem to care. We're from a little town called Clewiston Fl, people raping their kids and getting away with it. People are being abused and beat yet people sweep it under the rug as if nothing happened, and the kids are too afraid to speak up cause the parents just get mad and say you lying, hell for all I know you tried him. My husband said so bae keep going then, I'm going to support you if no one else does. So, I had to keep moving forward. My family I love they support me so much I love y'all.

Remember: you cannot help anyone who doesn't want to be helped, and you can't force anyone to get help. They have to be willing and ready for themselves.

Thanks for reading my novel

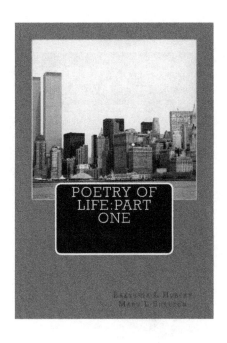

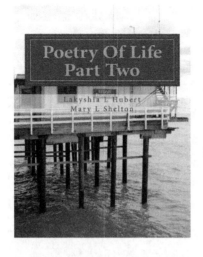

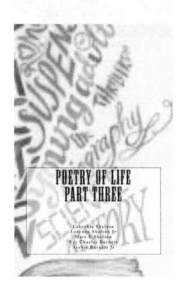

A CHILDREN'S BOOK
TO LEARN, COLOR,
PLAY & SEARCH!

Sex In The
Strangest Places

Lakyshia L. Hubert

SEX IN THE AIR

Let's Get Buck Wild

Lakyshia L. Shelton

Made in the USA
Columbia, SC
27 February 2024

31958646R00055